D1134165

Biographies of famous people to
support the curriculum.

William Caxton

by Harriet Castor
Illustrations by Peter Kent

FRANKLIN WATTS
LONDON•SYDNEY

NORFOLK
LIBRARIES & INFORMATION SERVICE

839175

PETERS	20-Oct-00
686.2	£7.99

First published in 2000 by
Franklin Watts
96 Leonard Street
London
EC2A 4XD

Franklin Watts Australia
14 Mars Road
Lane Cove
NSW 2066

© 2000 text Harriet Castor
© 2000 illustrations Peter Kent

The right of the author to be identified
as the author of this work has been asserted.

The right of the illustrator to be identified
as the illustrator of this work has been asserted.

Front cover illustration: Nick Ward

ISBN: 0 7496 3679 3

Dewey Decimal Classification Number: 686.2

A CIP catalogue record for this book
is available from the British Library.

Series editor: Sarah Ridley
Historical consultant: Barbara Searle

Printed in Great Britain

William Caxton

Almost six hundred years ago,
a boy called William Caxton
was born in Kent, England.
No one is sure exactly where
he was born, or when, or who
his parents were. If anyone
wrote it down, the paper or book
they wrote on has been lost.

Many books from that time have disappeared. There were far fewer books then than there are today, and not many copies were made.

Making books was a slow job.
Each page had to be copied
out, word by word. The people
who did this, called scribes,
quite often made mistakes too.

Although we don't know much about William's childhood, we do know that when he was about 14, his parents sent him to live in the household of a rich merchant called Robert Large.

I will train you, and give you food and clothes. You must work hard.

William became Robert's
apprentice. This meant he
promised to work for Robert
until he was ready to be a
merchant in his own right.

Merchants made their living by buying and selling things. Often they took English goods abroad and brought things back from other countries to sell at home.

Many London merchants – or 'mercers' – were members of a powerful guild called the Mercers' Company. A guild was like a club for people who did the same job. Members looked after one another, and made rules about how the job should be done, to make sure it was done well.

When William was old enough, he joined the Mercers' Company. He began visiting towns abroad, such as Bruges (which is now in Belgium). There you could buy things not just from Europe, but from

places as far away as Egypt too. Mostly, William sold English woollen cloth, and bought luxuries to sell to rich people back home. Some of these luxuries were books.

Since books took so long to make, they were very expensive, and only wealthy people could afford to buy them.

Many books were highly decorated too. The words were beautifully written, with fancy capital letters which sometimes had tiny paintings inside.
The pages were usually made of vellum, a kind of animal skin. The outside, or binding, was often edged with gold.

Pro Sanctissimus et Deus

PAULVS

Gloria in excelis
Deo et in eterna
Et in terra pax
hominibus te.
Benedicimus
te. Adoramus
te. Glorificamus
te. Gratias agi
mus tibi propter
magnam gloria.

sianus
diem et
dominus
horus
nunquit
et tibi
praeto
luxit.
Semper
fideles
et vox
pater

William did well at his job, buying and selling cloth, books and other goods. As the years went by he became a rich and well-known merchant.

In Bruges, merchants from different countries had their own halls and churches, and each group chose a leader, called a 'governor'. When he was about 40 years old, William was made Governor of the English merchants at Bruges.

As Governor, William had to spend a lot of his time having meetings with merchants from other countries. The king of England, Edward IV, asked him to represent England at other meetings too.

This is William Caxton, King Edward of England's man.

Being Governor made William a very important person, welcome at the royal court. But after seven or eight years, he gave up the job. No one is quite sure why.

Perhaps it was because of trouble in England. For many years, two parts of the royal family had been fighting for the crown. This is now called the Wars of the Roses.

William supported Edward IV's side, the Yorkists. But now Edward had been pushed off the throne and his enemies, the Lancastrians, were in charge. Maybe the merchants wanted a Lancastrian governor instead of William.

Since he was no longer Governor, William decided to add a new branch to his business. Instead of just selling books, he decided that he would make them too.

But William wasn't planning to become a scribe. He wanted to learn a new trade that had begun to spread across Europe: printing.

I have enough money – I can set up a press of my own.

Printing wasn't a new idea.
But a new way had been found
to do it. Before, a whole page of
a book had been carved onto a
wooden block. This took a long
time, and every page needed a
new carving.

Now a way had been found
to print using separate metal
letters. For each page, the letters
could simply be rearranged.

You need a special sort of ink that spreads evenly over the metal.

With this new method, invented by a man called Johannes Gutenberg, books could be made far more quickly and cheaply. In the time it took a scribe to make one copy, a printing press could make hundreds.

William was a clever businessman; he realised that books would now become very popular, since more people would be able to afford them.

Black Letter

William learnt how to print
in a place called Cologne, in
Germany. No one is sure who
taught him, but his training
probably cost him lots of money.

Before he left Cologne William bought the equipment he needed to set up his own press. He hired trained workers too, and took them back to Bruges.

William decided to print his first book in English. This had never been done before. He chose a French book called *The History of Troy*, and translated it into English himself.

William hoped to sell his book to English nobles at the court of the Duke of Burgundy (who ruled Bruges). He also wanted to send books to England and sell them there.

29

Meanwhile, Edward IV had become king of England again. Even though William wasn't Governor of the merchants any more, Edward still gave him important work to do.

King Edward needs my help.

When an attack on France was planned by Edward and the Duke of Burgundy, William travelled around the Duke's lands, collecting five hundred ships to use in the attack.

All this travelling meant that
William could not operate
his printing press himself.
He decided what should be
printed and organised the selling
of the books, but he often left
the running of the press to his
assistant, Wynkyn de Worde.

While William was away
organising the ships for King
Edward, his second book,
The Game of Chess, was printed.

Selling books in England wasn't as easy to organise from Bruges as William had hoped. So, after a few years, he moved his press to London. He rented a shop next door to Westminster Abbey.

It was very near the king's Palace of Westminster, the Parliament and the main law courts. Nobles, courtiers and wealthy city people passed by every day.

Nobles and courtiers were more likely to buy a book if it had the support of a famous person, or 'patron'. In Bruges, the Duke of Burgundy's wife, Margaret, had sometimes been William's patron. She was King Edward IV's sister.

Now, in London, William found new patrons among the relatives of Edward's wife, Elizabeth.

The trouble was, the Wars of the Roses were not over. When Edward died, his brother seized the throne, and made himself King Richard III. But the Lancastrians wanted someone else to be king. There was a battle and Richard was killed.

Now William's important friends weren't important any more. He had to find new patrons.

In all, William put about a hundred different books into print. Some are still famous today, such as Geoffrey Chaucer's *Canterbury Tales*, and a book about King Arthur by Thomas Malory.

William carried on his
translating work, too.
Sometimes he wrote a few pages
of his own, to be printed at the
beginning or end of a book.

Meanwhile, printing had spread to many countries. Presses all over Europe and beyond were making far more books than ever before, and more and more people were learning to read.

Now not just priests and nobles but ordinary people too could read things for themselves. New ideas spread quickly, even between countries hundreds of miles apart.

In particular, printing was soon to pay a big part in changing religion in Europe. For the first time, bibles were printed in different languages so that ordinary people could read them.

William Caxton did not see all these changes. He died in 1491 or 1492, aged about 70. His printing press carried on, though. And his books carried on being read by hundreds of people.

Further facts

Printing and the new maps

Printing wasn't only used to make books. Pamphlets, notices, labels, documents and maps were also produced by the printing presses. Maps were changing a great deal at this time as explorers travelled to places no one from Europe had ever found before.

Printing in the East

Although printing was new to Europe in the 15th century, people in the East had been printing for hundreds of years before this. In China, printing with carved wooden blocks

was done in the 6th century. By the
11th century, Chinese printers were
using letters that could be moved.
It took Europeans another 400 years
to catch up, and
'invent' this method
for themselves.

Caxton's trade mark

Printing today

For hundreds of years, printers
carried on using the same basic
methods as Caxton. Then, in the
19th century, presses began to be
operated using steam power. Later,
ways were invented for typesetting
(the arranging of the letters) to be
done using a keyboard. Today
typesetting is done by computer.

Some important dates in William Caxton's lifetime

Between 1415 and 1424 William Caxton is born in Kent, England.

About 14 years later William becomes an apprentice of Robert Large, a successful London merchant.

Around 1444 William begins visiting Bruges regularly.

1452 William becomes a full member of the Mercers' Company.

1462 William becomes Governor of the English merchants at Bruges.

Between 1470 and 1472 William gives up being Governor and learns to print, probably in Cologne, Germany.

1472 William returns to Bruges and sets up his printing press.

1474-1475 William prints the first book ever printed in English, *The History of Troy*, which he has translated himself.

1476 William moves to England. He sets up his press in Westminster, London.

1478 William prints Geoffrey Chaucer's *Canterbury Tales*.

1491 or 1492 William Caxton dies.